The Ego and the Empiricist

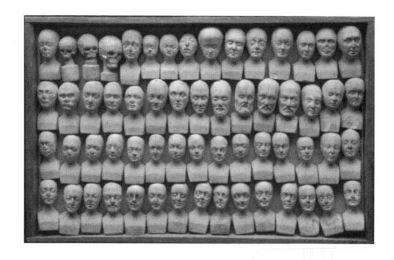

D0757246

Derek Mong

Finalist for the Two Sylvias Press Chapbook Prize

Two Sylvias Press

Two Sylvias Press
PO Box 1524
Kingston, WA 98346
twosylviaspress@gmail.com

Cover Design: Kelli Russell Agodon
Book Design: Annette Spaulding-Convy
Author Photo Interior: Wabash College
Cover Photograph: Bally's miniature phrenological specimens, England, 1831
                  (Science & Society Picture Library, London)

Created with the belief that great writing is good for the world, Two Sylvias Press mixes modern technology, classic style, and literary intellect with an eco-friendly heart. We draw our inspiration from the poetic literary talent of Sylvia Plath and the editorial business sense of Sylvia Beach. We are an independent press dedicated to publishing the exceptional voices of writers.

For more information about Two Sylvias Press or to learn more about the eBook version of *The Ego and the Empiricist* please visit: www.twosylviaspress.com

First Edition. Created in the United States of America.

ISBN: 978-0-9986314-3-1

Two Sylvias Press
www.twosylviaspress.com

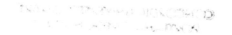

Praise for *The Ego and the Empiricist*

"Whatever I take from this forest floor," writes Derek Mong in this gorgeous new chapbook, "I borrow." And, true to this statement, Mong adeptly gathers a wide swath of source material and produces poems that honor their origins, spring off from them, and, ultimately, give back. As Mong explores the journey of the body over time, his lines are both charged and solemn, with turns of phrase at once unpredictable and spot-on. This is a haunting, riveting collection.
— Natalie Shapero

ॐ

A reader can open any contemporary journal of poetry and quickly pick up characteristics of the current mode. If the magazine is serious you'll also find good poems, and many more bad ones, and what falls between—the largest group. In this our age is like any other. Derek Mong's *The Ego and the Empiricist*, though its music is very much of our moment, takes as starting point poems and poets distant in time and worldview, and from first poem to last the difference is stunning. Mong has made of original medieval and renaissance works a grouping of wholly transformed new poems that sound contemporary, but retain the urgent intimacy of un-ironic spiritual "exercises," as the Jesuits might have it. As I read I began to think of these poems as a new species of *retablos*, with verbal objects in the place of iconic imagery. There is the same naïve, unmediated closeness of address to Christ—"You're smoke, you're/ thunder's anti-static rope," the same heuristic feel to the pieces, as if intentionally made for devotional purposes. How strange! Not since Lowell's *Imitations* (which Mong acknowledges in his notes) have we had a grouping of poems so alien in tone and tilt to the current secular mind brought into contemporary American idiom, fully alive, fully human. And human they are; these are not the words of the elevated or pious: "Still, I can't explain my fear/ of flies, nor the time I beat a man for smiling." There is everywhere an offhand grace, "Later a green glow, like the inside of a swept cape,/ hung where the sun crossed the bay," coupled always with the modesty of a true religious—"I am still building a theory for just what that means." I can hardly say how much I like these poems, which are shocking for all the unusual reasons.
— Jeffrey Skinner

ॐ

A poetry of transformation, *The Ego and the Empiricist* blurs the space between translation and homage, and shapes a free-ranging and symphonic landscape populated by monks, farmers, philosophers, bees, and all manner of amazements. In making lost voices come alive again, Derek Mong demonstrates the poet's most profound skill: the gift of speaking in tongues.
— Ann Townsend

Acknowledgements

Thanks to the following journals in which these poems first appeared, sometimes in slightly different forms::

American Literary Review: "Heliotrope, Or Man's Mind Angles Inevitably Toward God"

Artful Dodge: "In the Shadow of a Scrivener's Quill"

Colorado Review: "Litany" and "The Sun Is Our Ablest Meteorologist"

Drunken Boat: "Melancholia"

Laurel Review: "Hide and Seek"

minnesota review: "The Ego and the Empiricist"

Printer's Devil Review: "Blason Wherein My Head Becomes a Mountain" and "On the Flooding of Prague"

River and Sound Review: "Hadrian's Epitaph" (as part of "Heft")

The Southern Review: "The Rope Dancer," "The Coming of the Honeyed Age," and "The Later Psalms" (as "Latin Hymns").

"In the Shadow of a Scrivener's Quill" also appeared in *Redux* (online). "Heliotrope, Or Man's Mind Angles Inevitably Toward God" appeared in *Enclave* 7 (China) with accompanying Mandarin translations by Qin Sun Shu. "Melancholia" also appeared on *Drunken Boat's* Vintage DB blog (83).

The author would like to thank Wabash College and its Byron K. Trippet research fund for financial assistance in securing the cover image. Thanks as well to Kelli Russell Agodon and Annette Spaulding-Convy at Two Sylvias for their encouragement, professionalism, and hard work.

Table of Contents

Heliotrope, Or
Man's Mind Angles Inevitably Toward God

after Jacob Balde

No sliver of self   held in reserve, no

        life left but the one untangled from a sunray.

    I am a builder of footstools, crates.   I am countless nods

      begun in the direction of my last benediction.

My servitude must be verbally attested:

    I vow

to rake His heat into a Libyan beach, to let waves wash its glass curtains.

I vow to cut Carpathian surf with oars on loan from Homer.

    No jackknifed raft, no   cormorant (lured

        to me by the moon's dead eye) will delay

  my time inside His stain-glassed iris.

    The sins I've long messengered   He'll release

        as if speeding through a flipbook.

My friends,

    the North Pole's just one half of this archer's crosshairs.

  His quiver is limitless.

  All seek its acupuncture.

See them shuffle up and stand.   Their shadows follow like regimental backup.

They count

                    their wounds to four and fall away.

The rest kneel or bow.

We smaller targets prove Him the finer marksman.

Litany

after the Precatio Terrae

To know what part's raw merriment, what's wrath   released

    in season—   your geysers skywrite, they loop; a mudflow moves

        every trunk and tree root. Gaia, Arbiter of the All

  Natural, we are indefatigable   readers: a cirrus cloud

            is string to tease out storms; see stones in stream—

    we pray halfway through fording.   Once I met a man. He sailed.

    Claimed hurricanes were coins   you clicked across your knucklebones

or dropped, if distracted.

        We gardeners aren't so gullible. We've watched the surf toss

    a cliff's ledge like piecrust.   At whim

you'll turn your insides out—   your moods make

    my other gods a hobby.

        One day I'll relinquish weather signs

    and drift like pine needles within them.   I imagine myself

            inside both sea and sky, crashing the cheek

  of a slave girl. Diva, sweet Earth Queen—

I am an herb gatherer in search of my fair allotment.

Whatever I take from this forest floor   I borrow.

The Sun Is Our Ablest Meteorologist

after Giovanni Pontano

For years I've lived my life like a sundial, watching
as my shadow circles the town square.

My feet hold tight to the gallows. My head
leans against all your doors.
                              Here's what I've learned:

          If the noon sun dries the tide pools
          like broth pots

          then the south wind will misroute a river.
          Later, the marshes will fill with saltwater fish.

          Or say light rays strafe us
          as if passed through high prison bars—

          turn then to your war wounds.
          Swollen toes point to downpours;
                                        the hollow

          eye socket throbs, foreboding
          a fine crop of corn. It'll sprout unremarked.

For all who doubt me, remember the hailstorm.
I augured that disaster from the bell tower

you turn to for prayer.

          That day the sun lurched drunkenly, masked
          though it was by darkening clouds. Time

          and again, a lone
                            beam would drain

          the sky's soup, touch
          this house, that one, before sealing back up.

The penned sheep howled for mercy.

That night I ate lamb.
Likewise, the night after that.

Later a green glow, like the inside of a swept cape,
hung where the sun crossed the bay.

I am still building a theory for just what that means.

Hide and Seek

after Matthias Sarbiewski

Our whispers stricken, glances   thinned to sheets

        the sun anneals (one ounce love yields six gilded leaves)—

                till now, my Christ,   we're separate

           as comet from constellation. My pain's enflamed

           by your infinite expansion.

      You're smoke, you're   thunder's antistatic rope, coaxing

sparks up a tree trunk.   Meanwhile, the day makes skillets from our sundials.

        Next door, the farmer harvests popcorn.   I ask him: where did

                your departure whisk you?

The shepherd doesn't know. His trio (white flock, black   birds, black flies)

           lingers, exchanging places. A gap breaks

in a bank of clouds: your big toe testing the water?

           I ask the innkeeper, I ask

       the county priest.   Both balance drinks upon your dog-eared book

    but won't address my thirsting. Are you

        baked in sod, wearing

whiskered moss—   maybe you've woven a hammock

between the pine trees? My sweat

seeks your low ground. These sighs

travel the high plains

dodging windmills.

If you're perched atop one, wait: I'll walk

beneath your sandaled feet.

My lungs are large enough to spin the blades.   I'll glimpse you in their turning.

The Rope Dancer

after Vincenzo Guiniggi

Who's this—   some tightrope Daedalus? You scrape

heaven's lowest echelon,   then pause to flaunt a wingspan

grown exclusively for clotheslines. Know this:

your audience anticipates Icarus,

the taut string struck like a pizzicato note—   gravity come

wailing up to greet you.

I've slayed you a hundred times this morning—

when church bells rend the sky like cavalry; when

a gust kicks up—   but your dancing's buoyed by one glance

at the tightrope. Maybe you'll bed down

tonight, wake with your fellow hollow-boned: the sparrows.

Question: have our cheers brought you six floors

nearer to God   so you can imitate a hanged man?

Your chin's a coat hanger's hook; your toes point

like plumb bobs through these buildings.

Swaying once you eclipse our crucifix—

the rope drops like a voice inside a valley.

Is it not enough to playact pain? Do you   swap your earthly demise

for one inside a cloud's eye?

The Coming of the Honeyed Age

after Matthias Sarbiewski

Winged lace we lacerate, a good buzz   run asunder—

      are you, dear swarm, one or a hundred?

Yesterday, fields ablaze with sun, I traced

        grain stalks   and ceded thought

to your diffuse armada. My body soloed.

      But my nephews (they're farmers),

my nephew's children (gentle, flower-

      beheaders)   don't register that rarest

      of erasures. Separately, they thrash

pasture you begat   then sweeten their teacups.

      We reproduce and undo you.

The Ego and the Empiricist

after Nicolas Avancini

So you clock every errant star,   measure molten rock's

              viscosity with honey; you've mapped fields creasing

       near a stream's tear duct—   such pursuits I'm not averse to.

         Plant a forest floor atop these conifers and I'll be the first

to mole up and sun this tonsure.

              But inquiry shot through the mind's cavity

        just ricochets: we're less empirical   than tide charts.

                       Take me: I measure my neighbor's

wheat, track his wife's hours outdoors, and in what

          color headscarf.   Still, I can't explain my fear

of flies, nor the time I beat a man for smiling.

           Or look toward your soul—   go spelunking.

                  You'll find our predawn thoughts

puddled deep enough to chill your ankles.

         You'll find a stage to rehearse

              life's play before God   sucks the air

out of all the theaters. He points a finger up or down—

           that's where we give our encore.   Do you see

now that numbers

                    are as useful as fishing lures for Jonas?

I'll wait while you clap your erasers out—

                              my hands

seek (through these clouds   of chalk) your forehead.

Melancholia

after Jacob Balde

Dear Germany—
somewhere a cartographer spilled his inkwell.
It's been ten years
                              since your darkness crept up
and held me.
My jailer hands me one candle a week.

          Its flame hopscotches mountaintops
          before drowning in a fogbank.

          Meanwhile the moon's dull shield
          blunts the light these rolled sheets spyglass.

Once, from the high window
                                        bars, a crow's glassy eye
reflected my likeness. Imagine his eyes

transfixed by carrion. That's the furthest
my visage has traveled.

          Even starlight, ever chartable, won't lead me
          back to my hometown's

          stained glass. I've not the astronomy
          to constellate an exit.

And so I shall escape on a cellmate's lips,
this little song whispered on the gallows.

Does the hangman still lunch
                                        under the church bells?
So scared am I of the mildly deaf

that I dedicate these words
to anyone who'd read them into a windstorm.

I'll hold fast till they're cast
off—

    I want my song audible to ironmongers.

The Later Psalms

Peter Damian

Whose footfalls
                      are those

slowing just as the balled fists
thunder my door—
                              trumpet
through the night's silence

calling me?

           Oh you, only
you, beautiful sister,

hair damp and moonlit,
agleam like candlestick sterling

           you're returning,
                     exiled bride.

Just wait,
           I'll rise—

Welcome home.

Boethius

Here, yes here, where the road
ends in earthworks
                    and darkens,

here, if you look back and forget
the direction you've taken,

you can speak once, say,
                    "Yes, I remember,
this is my homeland—

I've scuffed my feet on these rocks
my mother once carried me over."

            And if you still wish
to reflect on the miles
                    and moonfalls

you've relinquished,
just bend your eyes to the horizon—

            where the men go,

leaving the wretched
to dry up

like yesterday's dew.

Peter Damian

Although my mind thirsts
for more years,
                    lifetimes

poured
through my skin

            like a fountain,

I know this skin
is but the hard flesh
my soul does what it can
                        to tear
asunder—

it swells like a storm cloud
when choirs sing,
                    shaking

the hollow bars
        of my rib cage

as one would a locked door.

How many years
must it suffer—
                    exiled

inside a vessel thinly translucent?
Only this mouth,
                    these ears

accept the song
of our Lord.

Alcuin

Come now, my Beloved, and leave
these songs
                to their cradles,

be they of grief or salvation,

remembering that one hymn
continues:
                our love song

is a harpsichord left
out for the wind.

Oh my Beloved,
although I write this verse weeping,
I believe in the Man

whose scarred palms could dry
both our eyes—

and then, as our tears
turn to pearls on his fingers,
                        we'll see

each other more clearly,
and then,
            oh Beloved,

may our chests heave
with the swell of his heart.

Blason Wherein My Head Becomes a Mountain

after Joachim Du Bellay

Although my dome's snow-capped

                and holds the balance of my living—

      although my yawn stretches these boot heels

         into the New World—   my flesh is still within reach

of my wife's imagination.

          To her my tongue   is a desert steppe which the simplest thoughts

              only limp across.   I can't slap

       myself hard enough to jar one loose

and disprove her.

      Seeking what's left of me   she finds only epithets and insults:

       my pulse is a lava flow—

          however hot it's not quick

enough to please her.   My back's a jungle she can't cut through.

    I once bought a hundred grains of rice

         on which she could describe   my decrepitude,

          then boil her distaste into our dinner.

But my bad looks are vast as the land itself—

      she can't sprinkle salt

    without filling one of my pockmarks.   And though consistently tread upon,

   I can't bear this life alone:

        I'm just not that kind of Atlas.

On the Flooding of Prague

after Elizabeth Jane Weston

Today the heads of weathervanes
pierced Heaven's belly.
                              Rain clouds rubbed
our sooty roofs. Their downpour grew

like a sinkhole—

> Soon the Moldau swelled, its streams
> wimpling like rain beads on glass.

> I watched a man, I watched his wife.
> She waved to me from their armoire.

> He rode a tree trunk down the side streets—
> fruit trailed like buoys from its boughs.

My neighbors never concerned me much
till the deluge threw
                              their front doors open.
Who then didn't give rain the right of way

  or let the waves drop in for dinner?

> They emptied the pantries
> and cleaned low-lying dishes.

> All the goblets were quickly refilled.

> The altars everywhere baptized
> themselves when the flood receded.

Those of us on upper floors could assume
a voyeur's indifference
                              until we spied ourselves,
at rain's end, in that watery stillness.

We saw fish in flowerpots.
We thought of the drowned, wide-eyed

and rising now, halfway up our stairwells.

Hadrian's Epitaph

Little naked soul, nomad with no
footpath—

you are both my body's air
and armor.

To what realm do you now go, little
sallow,

sulking soul, no longer accustomed
to our joking?

In the Shadow of a Scrivener's Quill

Over the *O,* the *ah,* the fable's lazy start, its *Once*
Upon a Time; over the gild-work and into the text block, past
the signatures and spine; over the names

remaindered from distant shores which you swept
up and relined; over the *we,* the *she,* the *I*; over
the cattle carts clacking on cobblestones,

dead prayers, lost plays, gun-free melees,
and the other sounds those foreign consonants retain—
over the footnotes, toward the fore edge, through

the marginalia that's raining down the vellum's white,
inviting frame; over the gaps which absent words
plant into the lines; over the cloth

that holds your place; over the ink that's dried;
over the flesh and under the hide of enough
animals it's said whole herds passed

through your hands; over the grooves
your newest word still shines inside, past the pages
bound face-to-face, revised; over the stories,

all the oldest ones, which—like light we skim
from distant stars—renders our hurtling less lonely;
over the eons, inside the authors, onto an easel

and into your inkwell, the shadow of your scrivener's quill
is dancing, dark foot dipped into a darker pool, it lifts
a load of sweet, unfiltered evening

then lands, black dash to reattach the past,
and coax us up the learning curve we climb
by generations. O monk or scribe

who curled his back inside candlelight, I've often
questioned your motives: did penitence push
you to push books into the dark beyond—

stepping stones you leapt toward St. Peter's ledger—
or was scribe work just an exercise in exercising options?
Take that candle for life's defining metaphor

and the tomes you shelve begin
to resemble heaven. Perhaps you were seduced
enough to change them, as when chaperones

left alone too long imagine misbehaving?
Or did anonymity only remind you
of the pleasures it offered in compensation: to live

for months inside Homer's head, bundled
up in one-word increments; to touch the word
of God, put it down in red, before returning

to a relay team that runs for centuries
untended? One day our world will call you up
again, place into your hands our scraps

of self, and ask you to arrange the parts
that make us sharp, redeeming. For now may you
swim inside our memory, rippling unnoticed.

Notes

The preceding poems are adaptations from Silver Age, Medieval, Jesuit, and Neo-Latin poets. Together they constitute "one voice run[ning] through many personalities, contrasts and repetitions" (Lowell, *Imitations*). They are not to be read as translations. My sources are as follows:

Jacob Balde (1604-68) was in the midst of serenading a woman when he heard the psalms in a nearby chapel. He joined the Jesuits shortly thereafter. For "Heliotropium, Sive Mens Hominis ad Deum Versa" and "Melancholia" see Nichols's *An Anthology of Neo-Latin Poetry* (1979).

The **Precatio Terrae**, an anonymous prayer, possibly Augustan, can be found in Duff and Duff's *Minor Latin Poets* (2 vols, 1935).

Giovanni Pontano (1429-1503) wrote a five-book astronomical poem (*Urania*) and a two-book poem on the cultivation of lemon trees (*De Hortu Hesperidum*). "De solis prognosticis" is from the former (see McFarlane's *Renaissance Latin Poetry*, 1980).

Matthias Sarbiewski (1595-1640) was, for the two centuries after his death, the best-known Polish poet in the world. He wrote about bees ("Ad Apes Barberinas") for Pope Urban VIII. See "Ad Iesum, Ex Sacro Salomonis Epithalamio" in Mertz, Murphy, and Ijsewijn's *Jesuit Latin Poets* (1989).

Vincenzo Guiniggi (1588-1603) entered the Society of Jesus at the age of 13 and worked for many years on a history of the Jesuits. He died deaf ("In Funambulum," Mertz, Murphy, and Ijsewijn).

Nicolas Avancini (1611-86) lived in Passau, Vienna, and Graz. He wrote plays for college students ("Ad Annaeum Feronium" Mertz, Murphy, and Ijsewijn).

Peter Damian (1007-73) was a Benedictine monk. Dante mentions him in the *Paradiso*. For "De Beata Maria Virgine" and "De Gloria Paradisi," see Corrigan's *More Latin Lyrics from Virgil to Milton* (1976).

Boethius (c. 480-524) was a Roman Consul who wrote his best-known work, *The Consolation of Philosophy*, while awaiting his own execution ("Huc te si reducem referat via," Corrigan).

Alcuin (c. 735-804) was a leader of the Carolingian Renaissance ("Carminis hic finem," Corrigan).

Joachim Du Bellay (1522-60) was a member of the Pleiade group, which sought to reform French poetry on classical models. He also died deaf ("Conversio Sui in Montem," Nichols).

Elizabeth Jane Weston (1581-1612) was the stepdaughter of a disgraced alchemist and the only woman to have published a book of Neo-Latin poems (for "De inundatione Pragae ex continuis pluviis exorta," see Churchill, Brown, and Jeffrey's *Women Writing Latin*, 3 vols, 2002).

Hadrian (76-138) was the Emperor of Rome and a friend of the poet Publius Annius Florus, with whom he exchanged work ("Animula vagula blandula," Duff and Duff).

Derek Mong is a poet, essayist, translator, and scholar. The Byron K. Trippet Assistant Professor of English at Wabash College, he has held the Axton Fellowship in Poetry at the University of Louisville and the Jay C. and Ruth Halls Poetry Fellowship at the University of Wisconsin. He also taught at the University of Michigan, SUNY-Albany, Stanford University, the Edna St. Vincent Millay Society, and with young writers workshops at Kenyon College and Denison University, his alma mater. He received an M.F.A. from the University of Michigan and a Ph.D. in American Literature from Stanford.

The author of two poetry collections from Saturnalia Books—*Other Romes* (2011) and *The Identity Thief* (forthcoming, 2018)—his work appears widely: the *Kenyon Review*, *Pleiades*, the *Southern Review*, the *Brooklyn Rail*, *Two Lines*, *Blackbird*, *Poetry Northwest*, *New England Review*, and elsewhere. He reviews new poetry for the *Gettysburg Review* and blogs at the *Kenyon Review Online*. His work has been anthologized in *99 Poems for the 99 Percent* (2014) and *Writers Resist: Hoosier Writers Unite* (2017). His awards include the *Missouri Review*'s Editor's Choice Prize, two Pushcart nominations, and the Artsmith Poetry Prize.

Born in Portland, Oregon and raised outside of Cleveland, he now lives in Crawfordsville, Indiana with his wife, Anne O. Fisher. Together they received the 2018 Cliff Becker Translation prize for their collaborative translation of the selected poems of Maxim Amelin (Russian, b. 1970): *The Joyous Science*. This project was awarded a 2010 NEA grant for Literary Translation. It is forthcoming from White Pine Press.

They are the parents of a young son.

Publications by Two Sylvias Press:

The Daily Poet: Day-By-Day Prompts For Your Writing Practice
by Kelli Russell Agodon and Martha Silano (Print and eBook)

The Daily Poet Companion Journal (Print)

Fire On Her Tongue: An Anthology of Contemporary Women's Poetry
edited by Kelli Russell Agodon and Annette Spaulding-Convy (Print and eBook)

The Poet Tarot and Guidebook: A Deck Of Creative Exploration (Print)

The Ego and the Empiricist, Finalist 2016 Two Sylvias Press Chapbook Prize
by Derek Mong (Print and eBook)

The Authenticity Experiment
by Kate Carroll de Gutes (Print and eBook)

Mytheria, Finalist 2015 Two Sylvias Press Wilder Prize
by Molly Tenenbaum (Print and eBook)

Arab in Newsland, Winner of the 2016 Two Sylvias Press Chapbook Prize
by Lena Khalaf Tuffaha (Print and eBook)

The Blue Black Wet of Wood, Winner of the 2015 Two Sylvias Press Wilder Prize
by Carmen R. Gillespie (Print and eBook)

Fire Girl: Essays on India, America, and the In-Between
by Sayantani Dasgupta (Print and eBook)

Blood Song
by Michael Schmeltzer (Print and eBook)

Naming The No-Name Woman,
Winner of the 2015 Two Sylvias Press Chapbook Prize
by Jasmine An (Print and eBook)

Community Chest
by Natalie Serber (Print)

Phantom Son: A Mother's Story of Surrender
by Sharon Estill Taylor (Print and eBook)

What The Truth Tastes Like
by Martha Silano (Print and eBook)

landscape/heartbreak
by Michelle Peñaloza (Print and eBook)

Earth, Winner of the 2014 Two Sylvias Press Chapbook Prize
by Cecilia Woloch (Print and eBook)

The Cardiologist's Daughter
by Natasha Kochicheril Moni (Print and eBook)

She Returns to the Floating World
by Jeannine Hall Gailey (Print and eBook)

Hourglass Museum
by Kelli Russell Agodon (eBook)

Cloud Pharmacy
by Susan Rich (eBook)

Dear Alzheimer's: A Caregiver's Diary & Poems
by Esther Altshul Helfgott (eBook)

Listening to Mozart: Poems of Alzheimer's
by Esther Altshul Helfgott (eBook)

Crab Creek Review 30th Anniversary Issue featuring Northwest Poets
edited by Kelli Russell Agodon and Annette Spaulding-Convy (eBook)

Please visit Two Sylvias Press (www.twosylviaspress.com) for information on purchasing our print books, eBooks, writing tools, and for submission guidelines for our annual chapbook prize. Two Sylvias Press also offers editing services and manuscript consultations.

Created with the belief that great writing
is good for the world.

Visit us online: www.twosylviaspress.com